ORVIS®

VEST POCKET GUIDE TO CADDISFLIES

The Orvis Fly-Fishing Guide,
full-color revised edition

The Orvis Vest Pocket Guide to Mayflies

The Orvis Vest Pocket Guide to
Leaders, Knots, and Tippets

The Orvis Vest Pocket Guide
to Terrestrials

The Orvis Guide to Prospecting for Trout,
full-color revised edition

The Orvis Fly-Tying Guide

THE

ORVIS®

VEST POCKET GUIDE TO CADDISFLIES

The Illustrated Reference to the Major Species of North America
Based upon *The Caddisfly Handbook*

Dick Pobst

The Lyons Press
Guilford, Connecticut
An imprint of The Globe Pequot Press

The Lyons Press is an imprint of The Globe Pequot Press.

Printed in China

10 9 8 7 6 5 4 3 2 1

Design by Sterling Hill Productions

Library of Congress Cataloging-in-Publication Data is
available on file.

ISBN 978-1-59228-391-0

In Memoriam

Carl Richards was born in 1933 and died on Memorial Day 2006. His death cost us one of fly fishing's most creative minds. He and Doug Swisher produced *Selective Trout*, possibly the most influential book in the history of fly fishing. They authored numerous other books, but this was their magnum opus.

Quite a few years later, Carl asked me what important subject in fly fishing would be worth a book. My reply was a book on caddisflies that was understandable, with appropriate photographs, and a determination of which hatches were important, and when they occurred. Carl then began a program of study to accomplish that. For a number of years he consulted with scientists, and spent many days fishing the caddisfly hatches and nights camped out on rivers so he could find out what caddisfly activity occurred around the clock. My part was to explore the caddisfly hatches in the Rockies. Those efforts resulted in *The Caddisfly Handbook*, upon which this book is based.

In terms of important practical entomology, this work stands high on Carl's long list of accomplishments.

—DICK POBST

CONTENTS

Acknowledgments

We would like to thank the many people who helped us in this venture: Dr. John C. Morse, Clemson University, for verifying the facts of this new edition. John Juracek and Craig Mathews, authors of *Fishing The Yellowstone Hatches*, for advice and slides. Dave Hughes, author of *Western Streamside Guide* and photographer, for advice and slides. Jim Schollmeyer, author of *Hatch Guide For Western Streams*, for slides of the insects. Thomas Ames, Jr., author of *Fishbugs*, an outstanding book for avid anglers, for coming up with some hard-to-find pictures. Tom Rosenbauer, author of *Reading Trout Streams* and the new *Orvis Fly-Fishing Guide*. Robert McKeon, artist and illustrator, who did the original black-and-white drawings in the previous version of this text. Alecia Richards, wife of the late Carl Richards, and Nancy Pobst, for their critiques and suggestions. The host of other anglers who helped us along the way.

Introduction

My coauthor on the previous version of this book, Carl Richards, started fishing Michigan's Muskegon River in 1959, and he introduced me to it in the mid-1970s. This river had terrific caddisfly hatches but no one could consistently catch fish, even when the trout were feeding on the caddis all around us.

Skunked a lot. When we did catch fish we took some fat, strong, well-conditioned trout, for the river is rich in caddisflies. Twelve-inch fish shaped like footballs would put up a great fight, and the larger 19-inch cruisers could keep anyone's adrenaline going all evening. There were plenty of fish, and plenty of bugs, but we could not sort out which flies the fish were taking, and we were frequently skunked.

Caddis and the Angler, by Larry Solomon and Eric Leiser, and *Caddisflies*, by Gary LaFontaine, provided considerable information—more information than we could actually process. *Caddisflies* listed some 193 species, a small portion of the existing species. We would certainly never learn to fish all these. For a long time it seemed that the more we learned, the more difficult the puzzle became.

We turned to academia to learn more about caddisflies. We found shelf after shelf of scholarly papers on the insects, but most of the papers provided little information about the color, size, or behavior of these flies. And they listed over 1,300 North American species, so the problem of sorting out the hatches got worse.

Finding the Really Important Hatches

A few years ago, we began to doubt there were many important hatches—that is, important enough for the fish to feed steadily and regularly on them. So we collected samples from the Muskegon River and sent them to Richard Merritt of the Michigan State University Entomology Department. This time we said: "We do not want an analysis of every insect—only those that occur in great numbers."

After a summer of submitting specimens, we got our answer. There are only two species of any real importance during the summer. Carl then began a more exhaustive study and confirmed that there are two major hatches on the Muskegon, plus a few of secondary importance.

After several seasons of continued investigation, we finally concluded that about four genera of caddisflies constitute up to three-quarters of the fishable hatches in the United States. There are a dozen of secondary importance, and probably no more than 50 species in the entire country of significance. Contrast that with the aforementioned 1,000 species, or even the 193!

The Importance of Behavior

Once we were able to narrow the list, we turned our attention to determining how to figure out to which stage of the insect life cycle we were fishing. This is far more difficult with caddisflies than with mayflies, and far more important. Mayflies undergo a physical change from dun to spinner, so one glance will tell you if you are fishing to an emergence or a spinner fall, but caddisflies do not change between emergence and egg laying. If you see a caddisfly on the water you won't know if it has just emerged from the pupa or if it's a female returning from the bottom after egg laying, because they look alike. Furthermore, many mayflies lay their eggs on the surface, while most caddisflies oviposit (lay eggs) underwater. We had to learn the habits of the various genera because their behavior can vary considerably, even though the forms may look alike. It is vital to know these differences to fish each successfully.

We learned that most caddisfly pupae swim to the surface using their middle legs in breaststroke fashion, but some crawl out of the water to hatch. Once reaching the surface, they may drift for considerable distances attached to the underside of the surface film, or they may break the surface film immediately and begin struggling out of their pupal shucks. The insects will drift from 5 to 30 feet during the struggle. A good pupal imitation is effective when the natural pupae are drifting under the surface, but an emerger is a killer when trout are feeding on emergers. Once the wings are out, most caddisflies flap them once or twice, then fly away. The adult pattern is thus less effective than a pupa or emerger because the natural adult is not easily available to the fish. However, the adult pattern is effective when the fish are feeding on adult females swimming back to the surface after egg laying.

Scientific Names or Common Names

Often the common names of the caddis are not widely used. Some are cumbersome, such as *dinky purple-breasted sedge*. Names like *sedge* and *grannom* have no specific meaning. On the other hand, Latin names are hard to remember, and they intimidate people. We have decided to include both; use the one you find more helpful. As for pronunciation of Latin names, just try your closest approximation of Italian or Spanish, as if reading a menu. Latin teachers, scientists, and priests all use different pronunciations. No one alive has ever heard a native speak Latin, so the next person does not know any more about it than you do. Besides, the names are not purely Latin; they're a mixture of Latin, Greek, and a whole lot of other things.

We have taken some liberties, however, with the common names. We have tended to use *tiny black caddis* for many #20 black caddis forms, since that is the way we first notice them, rather than *short-horn* or *weedy water sedge* names. We have used *long-horn* to distinguish those caddisflies with long antennae, since those antennae are their most obvious characteristic. And we have tended to prefer *tan caddis* to *spotted sedge*, because it seems more descriptive. In most cases we have given more than one name.

CHAPTER I

The Caddisfly Rivers

Much of our caddis research has focused on whether there is a pattern to where and when caddisflies reach major hatch proportions. We found that some rivers, such as the Muskegon in Michigan, are mainly caddisfly rivers. Much of the summer you must know the caddisflies to fish these rivers. Other rivers, however, such as the Clinch in Tennessee, are mainly mayfly rivers, with only a few caddis species. What is the difference? There is no single answer to this question that covers all streams.

Tailwaters

Caddisflies appear in significant quantities most often on tailwaters and large trout streams. This is important because most of the largest trout streams in the country are tailwaters. Michigan's Muskegon, Manistee, and Au Sable, below their dams, meet all the requirements, and they do have huge hatches of caddisflies. So do the Madison and Missouri in the West, as well as the great tailwaters of the Tennessee Valley Authority. We believe trout eat more caddisflies than mayflies in these tailwaters, but studies are rare and difficult to interpret.

Some rivers are fed by natural lakes and have great hatches of caddis; these should be classified with the tailwaters. The Yellowstone is a prime example. So one category of caddisfly rivers is warm-water tailwaters—rivers fed by top-spill dams or natural lakes.

When water is released from the base of the dam and where a deep reservoir of cold water exists, other tailwaters may have colder water temperatures, such as the Bighorn in Montana, and the South Holston and Clinch in Tennessee. These rivers produce more mayflies and fewer caddisflies than do warmer rivers. Temperature is undoubtedly a factor in determining which insects thrive in which places.

We believe the major factor, though, is that lakes—natural or artificial—produce large quantities of plankton near the surface; this plankton is fed into rivers by top-spill dams and natural lakes, but not so much from bottom-release dams. The most important caddisflies feed largely on plankton, and therefore thrive in the top-fed rivers. These are the Hydropsychidae, about which more will be said later.

In those cases where hydroelectric dams raise and lower water levels dramatically, this flushing action scours the river of organic material, so only the plankton eaters are likely to survive.

Trout Streams

There is one major group of caddisflies, however, that does not rely solely on plankton. This is the black caddisfly, or Mother's Day caddisfly (*Brachycentrus*). They thrive in cold water, and usually hatch during the cold early trout season. They are most common in undammed trout streams but will hatch in some tailwaters during spring periods of cold water.

Trout streams do not regularly produce the huge caddisfly hatches that occur in tailwaters, but there are significant hatches—which are frequently ignored by anglers because the mayfly hatches are so much easier to detect and analyze. As you become more familiar with the caddis populations of your trout streams, you will find many more opportunities to fish them.

Small, woodsy brook trout streams produce few mayflies but lots of caddisflies. The brook trout in these streams consume more caddisflies than mayflies.

Spring Creeks

The classic spring creeks, such as those of the Yellowstone Valley, produce huge quantities of mayflies and far fewer caddisflies. Their colder water and decreased amount of plankton are probably factors.

No Two Rivers Are Alike

It is really necessary to analyze each river separately, because most rivers do not fit neatly into a simple category. For example, the Henry's Fork is fed by both springs and lakes, and has variations in gradient and structure that make it difficult to categorize. It also hosts just about every kind of fly known to anglers. Don't try to oversimplify.

The Muskegon

A few years ago Michigan became the first state in which it was necessary to relicense major hydroelectric dams. This process fell under the jurisdiction of the Federal Energy Regulatory Commission, and would result in new licenses valid for 50 years. There have been huge conflicts between power companies and fisheries managers over the operation of the dams. This is a big story in itself.

Since we fish the Muskegon regularly, we were concerned about what would happen. We spoke to Gary Whelan of the Michigan Department of

Natural Resources, and asked him why they did not just leave the Muskegon alone.

Gary told us that if the dam operation was changed to natural-flow levels—run-of-the-river—rather than running in peaks to generate electricity, we would see huge increases in the production of aquatic insects. Constant, extreme fluctuations in water levels scour food from the water, so that only a few forms of aquatic insects can survive.

He said that equally important is the fact that frequently changing water levels provide no shallow-water nurseries for small trout, so they are eaten every time they are forced into the deep holes with the bigger fish.

The Muskegon's flow levels *were* changed, and both of Gary's predictions proved true. We now have more caddisflies, plus a burgeoning number of mayfly hatches—six new species at last count—and some stoneflies where they were rare before.

The Colorado River at Lee's Ferry has been through a similar process. It had few hatches when we fished it a few years ago, when water levels varied by several feet every day. We recently learned that the dam at Flaming Gorge Reservoir on the Green River no longer alters its levels so drastically, and understand that the insect hatches have improved considerably.

It seems that great improvements could be made in many tailwater fisheries if proper natural-flow regulations were implemented.

CHAPTER 2

The Life Cycle of the Caddisfly

The purpose of this book is to make the caddisflies understandable, and therefore fishable. Like love and marriage, you can't have one without the other. To fish caddisfly hatches, you need to understand the caddisfly life cycle.

Female caddisflies lay eggs on objects above the water on the water surface; by hitting the surface and diving to the bottom; or by crawling to the river's edge or onto pilings, then crawling to the bottom. It

Caddisfly larva: *Hydropsyche* (note three plates behind head)

Caddis pupa

is most important for the fisherman to observe which
genera use which methods of laying eggs.

The behavior of the larvae is complicated enough
to be the subject of an entire book, but a few points
are of major importance to the angler.

The most numerous flies are the Hydropsychidae,
which build nets to trap food. Most of the other
major genera build cases. The exceptions are the
Rhyacophilidae and some relatively minor families.
Caddisflies have the ability to spin silklike fibers
from their mouths. They use these fibers to build
cases like cocoons, to build webs, or to rappel from
one spot to another. The Hydropsychidae hatch
during the warm months, all over the country.

Caddis deposits eggs on water. Caddis dives to lay eggs then ascends. Spent caddis floats on surface.

Illustration by Robert McKeon

8   *The Life Cycle of the Caddisfly*

Caddis pupa swimming to the surface and emerging as an adult.

Illustration by Robert McKeon

Caddisfly case of *Brachycentrus*

Second most numerous are the Brachycentridae, which build chimney tube cases. When you see many of these cases in the early weeks of the season, there will be good hatches.

There are times when trout grub for larvae on the bottom. But the flies are only available in quantity during what scientists call behavioral drift, and during the cycle of emergence–egg laying–dying. Richard Merritt and Ken Cummins, noted entomologists, stated in a letter: "Feeding activity of trout occurs in connection with two major events: 1) the emergence behavior of aquatic insects, including the preemergence drift of nymphs and emerging adults, and egg-laying adults; and 2) during the major (dawn and dusk) drift periods."

Most behavioral drift occurs just before dawn and just after dusk. Usually the drifting larvae are without cases. A drifting larva floats with its head down, so we suggest a beadhead fly, fished dead drift with a strike indicator, during the drift period.

All caddisfly larvae turn into pupae to hatch. They do this either by sealing themselves in their existing cases, or by building a pupal case if they have no other. If you find caddisflies in sealed cases, they are going to emerge soon.

It is when the insects leave the pupal case and begin to emerge that the feeding cycle most exciting to anglers begins. Each stage of the emergence cycle causes the flies to be available in quantity and triggers major feeding activity by fish.

Some pupae drift along the bottom at first. These can be imitated by a pupa fished dead drift with a strike indicator.

All pupae eventually swim upward, using their legs to breaststroke their way to the surface. This is the point at which a pupa tied with a few strands of sparse soft hackle works well; fish it upward and with movement to make the legs swim. They do not rocket off the bottom—they swim slowly. They only rocket off the surface.

When the pupae arrive at the surface they frequently appear to drift just beneath the surface film, so close they are almost touching. In many cases their backs are actually attached to the surface film. This is the first stage at which the flies are collected into one spot in quantity and (from the fish's perspective) silhouetted against the sky. At this point they are extremely vulnerable to fish. Their legs, wings, cases, and antennae are visible under their bodies. The pupae appear practically inert, in what we call the tuck position.

Mating caddisflies

In most cases the pupae drift for several feet. This is their most vulnerable stage. In others they quickly work through the surface film and struggle to escape the pupal shuck. At such times, we fish a pupa tied as an emerger with or without a shuck attached.

In any event, as soon as the flies are free of their shucks, they quickly fly away. They are not readily available to fish as emerged adults.

After the flies reach the streamside bushes they mate without further change, and the females return to the river to lay their eggs. A female may lay eggs two, three, or more times during her life. An adult caddis pattern fished under the surface film or on the surface, depending on the egg-laying method in question, will work at this stage.

Finally, after laying eggs for the last time, the females fall spent on the surface. We have experienced major feeding activity on spentwing caddis after dark or at dawn during the Hydropsychidae season.

Spentwing caddisfly

The fish feed in calm, flat water and are extremely selective. There have been times when the only way we could hook a fish was to set the hook in anticipation of the strike. Here is how it works: When a fish is feeding selectively and rising in the same spot, make a mental note of the spot, no matter that the ring of the rise drifts downstream. Then cast a foot upstream of the spot. At the instant the fly drifts within an inch of the spot, raise the rod. With luck, the fish will take the fly just as you tighten the line. Otherwise, the fish would spit out your fly before you could set the hook. We have never figured out why they will reject so quickly sometimes and take so solidly at others.

Now you need to discover which insect you are fishing, so that you can make your fly act like the natural.

When you are uncertain whether the fish are taking the pupa, the emerger, or the adult that has just laid eggs, fish an adult caddis with a floating pupa dropper. If the fish fail to take either, tug the line to sink the dry fly and it will imitate the emerging egg layer.

CHAPTER 3

Identifying the Caddisflies

To understand caddisflies, concentrate on two facts.

First, two groups of flies make up the vast majority of significant caddisfly hatches: the black caddisfly of the springtime (*Brachycentrus*) and the tan caddisfly and its cousin, the little olive caddisfly, of the summertime (Hydropsychidae).

Second, the significant hatches of North American trout streams can be boiled down to about 20 genera, all of which are easily identifiable from their cases, or from their larvae if they have no cases. Probably no more than a half dozen are significant on your stream.

Once you recognize those 20 larval forms, you can tell what caddis hatches will occur in your waters.

First, Identify the Larvae or Cases

Stick to those specimens that are numerous. (Blank hatch charts, which can be copied, are printed on pages 112–123, and you can list any numerous specimens you find.)

Start by picking up rocks and logs to find the cases of larvae, which are mainly attached thereto.

Then seine gravel—the same way you would for mayfly nymphs, but with a few refinements. Seining will collect the caddisflies that do not build cases.

Tan Caddisfly and Little Olive Caddisfly
Family Hydropsychidae

Our estimate is that these flies may equal 40 to 50 percent or more of the fishable caddis. Concentrate on these first groups and your time will be well spent. This is the most complicated set of flies, scientifically speaking, but it boils down to two important ones:

1. The tan or cinnamon caddis (aka spotted sedge)—#16 hook—genus *Hydropsyche* (sometimes called *Ceratopsyche*).
2. The little olive caddis—#18 hook—genus *Cheumatopsyche*.

All these flies are easily identified if you remember that the larva has three dark plates on the first three body segments behind its head (see illustration). Also note the gills under abdomen.

This group is composed of closely related members of the family Hydropsychidae. They are the most important of all caddisflies and dominate in the summer months, especially on tailwaters and large rivers, although they are also found on smaller streams. The larvae can be easily captured by seining riffles.

The pupae emerge in midstream. Females lay their eggs either by swimming underwater (more than half) or by sprawling and bouncing on the surface. The adults can be identified by the straight trailing edge of their forewings. It is the predominance, similar behavior, and daytime emergence of these flies that make them so important. Two hook sizes and two colors imitate them all.

These flies build nets among the gravel to trap food, which consists of plankton. Plankton is mostly produced in lakes, above dams, and in warm-water pools in big rivers. This central fact accounts for Hydropsychidae being the most numerous flies in tailwaters and rivers fed by lakes.

Additionally, they are among the few flies than can survive in rivers where water levels are drastically raised and lowered, an action that wipes out the habitat of many other aquatic insects.

Little Black Caddisfly
Genus *Brachycentrus*

In all parts of North America, early black caddisflies hatch from chimney tube cases, as pictured. They are typically imitated with #16 hooks.

   In both East and West the black caddisfly is the first major caddisfly hatch of the season. This is the Mother's Day caddisfly of the Rocky Mountains and the black caddisfly of the East, and it creates major fishable hatches. *Brachycentrus* usually lay their eggs on the surface, like mayflies. They hatch most prevalently on undammed trout streams and bottom-release tailwaters because they need clear, cold water to survive. In each section of the country the initial hatch is followed by one or more relatives that live in the same sort of cases and same type of water. We estimate that these flies constitute around 20 percent of the fishable caddisflies.

Green Sedge
Genus *Rhyacophila*

This caddis is generally more important as a larva than as a dry fly. The green worms are often large and are an important part of the trout's (especially the steelhead's) diet. This caddisfly is so widespread that it cannot be ignored. It is the only major free-living caddisfly. It is easy to collect and identify. It can be distinguished from the *Hydropsyche* by the one light amber plate on the body segment behind its head, as compared to three dark ones. It usually does not emerge in a concentrated fashion, but egg-laying flights are sometimes massive and important. The females crawl underwater to oviposit. Emerging flies and escaping egg layers often skitter to shore after reaching the surface.

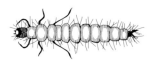

Most of the other major caddisflies are readily identified by the cases in which they spend most of their lives. When you visit a new river, you can determine which caddisfly hatches will be occurring by finding the cases or larvae. Following are illustrations you can use for that purpose. These can further by lumped into three categories:

Tiny Black Caddisfly

NAME		WHERE FOUND
Short-Horn Sedge *Glossosoma nigrior, G. montana*		E M W
Little Grannom *Micrasema bactro, M. rusticum*		E M W
Speckled Peter *Helicopsyche borealis*		E M W

Long-Horn Sedges

Long-Horn Sedge *Oecetis avara, O. disjuncta*		E M W
Black Dancer *Mystacides alafimbriata,* *M. sepulchralis*		W
White Miller *Nectopsyche albida*		E M
Dark Long-Horn Sedge *Ceraclea transversa*		E

Others

NAME	WHERE FOUND
Dark Blue Sedge *Psilotreta labida*	E
Grannom *Brachycentrus americanus*	E M W
Little Brown Sedge *Lepidostoma pluviale*	W
Weedy Water Sedge *Amiocentrus aspilis*	W
Dot-Winged Sedge *Neophylax fuscus*	E M
Great Brown Autumn Sedge *Pycnopsyche guttifer*	E M
Giant Orange Sedge *Dicosmoecus*	W

E=East; M=Midwest; W=West

Second, Identify the Adults

This will be easier if you have already identified the larvae or cases. For example, if you find a tiny black caddisfly and you already know *Glossosoma* cases are present in large numbers, you can deduce that this is what it is. Always catch the fly—never try to identify it in the air. To do so:

1. Use a fine-mesh net to strain the surface for emergers or egg layers. This may be a slow process; they are often widespread. What you catch, however, is probably what the fish are eating right now.
2. Use a long-handled net to sweep the grass and bushes along the stream. If a big hatch has occurred lately, you will easily capture many individuals.
3. Use a light trap at night to collect adults. Or make one, using a pan of alcohol covered with cooking oil under a light. Or just look in spiderwebs on buildings with lights on along rivers at night.
4. Carry a specimen bottle with acetone in it. The acetone will kill your specimen, so it cannot escape, while preserving its color.

Now use the cases, larvae, or adult specimens to find the correct fly in the following pages, which are organized by importance first in the West, then in the East.

For example, let's say you've found a bunch of cases in the river that look like this:

Page through the hatch chapters to find this case. When you do, you'll also find information about a hatch that will occur in your river this season (see page 36).

If you have a specimen of the adult, such as this one:

Helicopsyche borealis

You know that the hatch you predicted is happening now.

CHAPTER 4

Major Caddisflies
West of the Mississippi

The western states have many miles of major rivers that are suitable for trout. Many of these rivers are dammed. Therefore, caddisflies are probably more important here than they are in the eastern part of the country.

Most of our hatch dates come from rivers in the Yellowstone region, including the Yellowstone, the Henry's Fork, and the Missouri. Hatches in higher elevations will be later than on the Yellowstone. Hatches at lower elevations will be earlier—in the Pacific Northwest, for example.

Also note that some hatches in the mountain states will be unfishable in the early season; the high water of snowmelt will take these rivers out of the running.

Nevertheless, a huge portion of the great trout fishing in the world is to be had in the American West.

Western caddisflies are presented here approximately in their order of hatching. It also happens that the first flies listed are the most important. These are color-coded red. The next most important are coded blue, and the rest yellow.

Mother's Day Caddisfly (Black Caddisfly)
Family: Brachycentridae

Brachycentrus occidentalis–
Peak: April–mid-May.

B. americanus–Peak: Late
July–August.

These flies emerge in April and
May at midday, from cold-water
trout streams and cold tailwaters. Their characteristics are:

Brachycentrus occidentalis

HOOK #16 (males
one size smaller).

OVERALL LENGTH
8–13 millimeters.

BODY Dark gray with green or
tan lateral line.

Brachycentrus americanus

WINGS Gray with black veins.

LEGS Gray.

ANTENNAE Dark gray with
lighter rings.

Note: *B. americanus* has a
brownish cast and is larger (at
12–15 millimeters) than *B. occidentalis*. Its hatch peaks in late
July, early August.

Brachycentrus case: The case of the little black caddisfly is known as a chimney case. It has a square cross section and is tapered. The cases can be found clinging to stones and wood; they are numerous before the hatch.

Range: W, NW.

Habitat: Rocks or wood in cold trout streams.

Emergence: Midstream, midday.

Egg laying: Dips eggs on the surface in the afternoon.

The pupa, shown in the tuck position (next page), often drifts many feet attached to the surface film before emerging.

Artificial flies: See page 100.

This is the year's first heavy emergence of caddisflies in the West, and trout feed heavily on it. The hatch usually occurs on undammed trout streams and bottom-release tailwaters. The flies begin emerging around midday, just before runoff begins. Egg laying is in the afternoon and can coincide with the emergence. Peak emergence occurs from the last half of April to mid-June, depending on the river. The adults drift up to 30 feet struggling from their pupal shucks. Once out, they may drift on the surface or fly away quickly. They oviposit much like mayflies, dipping their bodies onto the surface, although some individuals may crawl or dive underwater.

Brachycentrus pupa

Spotted Sedge (Cinnamon or Tan Caddisfly)
Family: Hydropsychidae

Hydropsyche (Ceratopsyche) cockerelli, H. occidentalis, H. oslari, H. placoda, et. al.

Hydropsyche cockerelli

Hydropsyche adult

This is the most important caddisfly during summer months— Peak: All season; mostly afternoon and evening, but sometimes in the morning.

We prefer the name cinnamon caddisfly or tan caddisfly as more descriptive, since spots are not always evident.

These flies emerge from May to September, mainly during the evening in summer, but some earlier in the day. They are most important in tailwaters, but many are found in trout streams. Their characteristics are:

HOOK #16 (males one size smaller).

OVERALL LENGTH 9–13 millimeters.

BODY Cinnamon brown.

WINGS Brownish gray with a speckling of small tan spots.

LEGS Brown.

ANTENNAE Tan with dark rings.

Hydropsyche larva: This larva is characterized by three dark plates on the body segments behind its head, as are its relatives in the family Hydropsychidae.

It builds a net like a spiderweb among the gravel to trap food. It does not build a case until it is ready to pupate, about two weeks before emergence.

Range: W, NW.

Habitat: Gravel riffles; most prolific on tailwaters.

Food: Builds a net to strain plankton from lakes.

Emergence: Midstream, mostly afternoon and evening.

Egg laying: Crawls or dives to the bottom, or sprawls on the surface.

Hydropsyche adult

Hydropsyche larva
(note three plates behind head)

Artificial flies: See page 101.

This is by far the most important family for trout fishermen. Only in the early spring when little black caddisflies are on the water do any other caddisflies even come close in importance to this fly and its cousin, the little olive caddisfly.

They hatch in large numbers, usually in the evening but also in the morning, seemingly when the nights are very warm. Egg laying is done in the morning and evening, with some during the daytime.

Hydropsyche pupa: The emerging pupa, shown in the tuck position, often drifts many feet under the surface film while emerging.

These caddisflies may drift as pupae for a long time before their emergence. They also take a long time to struggle from their pupal shucks. These two factors allow you to hook a lot of fish long before the hatch begins on a pupal imitation fished dead drift on the bottom, as a floating pupa just under the surface film, or as an emerger. The pupae emerge in midstream.

The females crawl or dive underwater or sprawl on the surface to lay eggs. A surface-fished dry fly is often effective during egg laying, or it can be pulled under the surface to imitate the returning egg-laying female.

Many spent caddisflies collect on the water after dark, and the fish will feed selectively on quad-wing patterns during that time.

To find out which stage of the insect the fish are taking; tie on a floating fly; then tie a dropper from it and attach an emerger; then add a pupal imitation that will float just under the surface. Fish these dead drift. If the fish take one consistently, you know which fly to use.

Triple dropper rig

If the fish rise all around your flies but do not take, pull the dry fly underwater. It may then be taken for an egg-laying female returning to the surface.

Spotted Sedge
(Cinnamon or Tan Caddisfly)

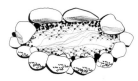

Temporary case (open on the bottom, attached to rock)

At the end of egg laying, fish will often take a spent imitation. A quad-wing fly or delta-wing fly will then work.

Note: Those caddisflies that do not live in cases as larvae—such as this one—build cases briefly for a couple of weeks to change into pupae. You can easily tell one of these pupal cases from the normal larval case because it is open on one side, exposing the silk-encased pupa. When you take a knife and remove it from a rock, the entire pupa is exposed as if in a window (see illustration). *Rhyacophila* builds a similar case, but has a golden cocoon around the pupa inside its case.

Little Sister Sedge (Little Olive Caddisfly)
Family: Hydropsychidae

Cheumatopsyche analis, C. lasia, C. campyla—Peak: All season, mainly afternoon and evening, but morning in fall.

These flies emerge from May to September, mainly during the evening in summer, but some earlier in the day. They are most important in tailwaters, but some are found in trout streams. Their characteristics are:

Cheumatopsyche lasia

HOOK #18 (males one size smaller).

OVERALL LENGTH
7.5 millimeters.

BODY Olive.

WINGS Brownish gray with a speckling of small tan areas.

LEGS Brown.

ANTENNAE Tan with dark rings.

Range: W, NW.

Habitat: Gravel riffles; most prolific in tailwaters.

Cheumatopsyche larva:
This larva is characterized by three
dark plates on the body segments

Food: Plankton from warm tailwaters.

Emergence: Midstream.

Egg laying: Crawls or dives to the bottom, or sprawls on the surface.

The pupa often drifts many feet attached to the surface film before emerging.

Artificial flies: See page 101.

This is the second most important genus for trout fishermen during summer months, a close second to *Hydropsyche*, to which it is closely related. Since these genera belong to the same family their habits, style of emergence, and egg laying are very similar, if not identical. They hatch and lay eggs at the same time of day, interspersed with the spotted sedge hatch.

These insects are similar in shape to spotted sedges and have the same unique wing shape. They are a little smaller than *Hydropsyche*, and can easily be distinguished from them by their smaller size and olive body color. The few

Hydropsyche that have olive bodies at emergence (which quickly turn cinnamon or brown) are larger. These caddisflies become much lighter as the season progresses—as do many other species, but the little sister seems to exhibit this trait in the extreme. The wings, which are dark in the early season, become much lighter in the fall and appear white in flight. They emerge in the morning and evening, but can come at midday on cool, overcast days. Ovipositing is usually at dusk in the West.

Temporary case (open on the bottom, attached to rock)

The females dive underwater or sprawl on the surface to lay eggs. A surface-fished dry fly is often effective during egg laying, or it can be pulled under the surface to imitate the returning egg-laying female.

Many spent caddisflies collect on the water after dark, and the fish will feed selectively on quad-wing patterns at that time.

Tiny Black Caddisfly (Short-Horn Sedge)
Family: Glossosomatidae

Glossosoma montanum—Peak: Spring and fall.

Glossosoma montana adult

Glossosoma case

These flies emerge sporadically from spring to fall in trout streams, occasionally in large numbers, usually in the morning.

HOOK #20
(males one size
smaller).

OVERALL LENGTH
6–7.5 millimeters.

BODY Black.

WINGS Black with a few light tan spots midwing and a few at the wing tips.

LEGS Dark gray.

ANTENNAE Black with light tan rings.

Glossosoma case: This is known as a domed saddle case. The larva takes the case with it as it moves along the surface of rocks.

Range: W, NW.

Habitat: Cold streams.

Emergence: Riffles, midstream.

Egg laying: Late afternoon, evening; dives in riffles.

Artificial flies: See page 100.

This is an important species because its members emerge all season long, usually a few at a time but occasionally in good numbers. They can cause heavy feeding when the emergence is large, and some rises when the hatch is light. Since these are small, dark forms, they are hard to see, but fish will feed on them. (You may notice that the trout are rising, but see nothing on the water.) The most important time for this hatch is during spring mornings, because not much else is emerging at this time.

The pupae emerge in midstream, and pupal and emerger imitations are effective. In the spring some pupae emerge in midstream and crawl on the surface of the water to shore. A hackled pupal imitation skittered on the surface is very effective at these times. Females submerge to oviposit.

Tiny Black Caddisfly
(Weedy Water Sedge, Little Grannom)
Family: Brachycentridae

Micrasema rusticum—Peak (Yellowstone); late July–early August.

Amiocentrus aspilus—Peak (Bighorn); Spring and fall.

Micrasema rusticum

Amiocentrus aspilus

These caddisflies hatch from cold-water trout streams during June evenings. The Bighorn has emergences in May and September.

HOOK #20
(males one
size smaller).

OVERALL LENGTH
7–9 millimeters.

BODY Dark gray with green lateral line.

WINGS Black.

LEGS Dark gray.

ANTENNAE Dark gray with lighter rings.

Range: W, NW.

Habitat: Cold streams.

Emergence: Midstream.

Egg laying: Crawls or dives; lays green egg balls.

Artificial flies: See page 100.

Micrasema case

These are important species because they emerge all season long, in good numbers. They cause heavy feeding when the emergence is large. Since these are small, dark forms, they are hard to see. (You may notice that the trout are rising, but see nothing on the water.)

Amiocentrus case

Another reason for the importance of these species is that the peak emergences in the West are concentrated and the caddisflies hatch in huge numbers, like the Mother's Day caddisfly, to which they are closely related. *M. rusticum* emerges and oviposits during warm summer evenings on the Yellowstone River in the park. *A. aspilus* is the important species on the Bighorn and has two emergence periods, one in May, the other in September. This hatch is a daytime affair and produces some heavy, but selective, feeding.

The pupae emerge in midstream and the adults fly off the water quickly, so a pupa or an emerger is the imitation of choice. Females crawl underwater or dip their bodies on the surface to lay eggs. The females that crawl underwater to oviposit swim back to the surface, where they float awash in the film. Adult imitations are best fished wet. Spentwing imitations should be used after egg laying.

Tiny Black Caddisfly (Speckled Peter)
Family: Helicopsychidae

Helicopsyche borealis–Peak: June-early July.

This caddisfly hatches from June to early July, in the evening, from all types of trout streams.

HOOK #20 (males one size smaller).

OVERALL LENGTH 7 millimeters.

BODY Bright amber.

WINGS Dark gray.

LEGS Gray.

Helicopsyche borealis

ANTENNAE Black with light gray rings.

Range: W, NW.

Habitat: Trout streams.

Emergence: Near banks.

Egg laying: On the surface near banks.

Artificial flies: See page 101.

Helicopsyche case

This is an important species because its emergence is concentrated, even though it is a small insect and often overlooked by fishermen. It emerges from mid-June to early July in the Rocky Mountain West, and early May to June on the Pacific Coast. This species prefers moderate currents rather than fast riffles. Emergence is in the evening in open water. Egg laying is also in the evening. The females either flop on the water when releasing their egg balls, or they crawl underwater from overhanging grasses, swim to the bottom, release the egg mass, and swim back to the surface. In either case, after ovipositing they ride the water in the normal resting position, drifting close to the bank, where trout unhurriedly sip them. The egg-laying flight is more important than the emergence. Even though these insects are small, they often emerge in numbers that can overshadow much larger insects like the green drake mayfly.

Green Sedge (Green Rock Worm)
Family: Rhyacophilidae

Rhyacophila bifila, R. coloradensis—Peak: Sporadic, spring to fall.

These caddis hatch spring to fall, in the evening, from fast, cold trout streams.

HOOK #14 (males one size smaller).

OVERALL LENGTH 12–15 millimeters.

BODY Green.

WINGS Grayish brown, mottled.

LEGS Tan.

ANTENNAE Tan with darker bands.

Range: W, NW.

Habitat: Cold-water riffles.

Emergence: Afternoon, from riffles.

Egg laying: Crawls or swims to the bottom in riffles.

Rhyacophila coloradensis

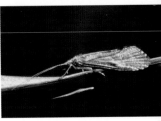

Rhyacophila adult

Green Sedge
(Green Rock Worm)

The green rock worm. Note the one hard plate behind the head— a characteristic of the *Rhyacophila*.

Temporary case (open on the bottom, attached to rock)

Artificial flies: See page 101.

This is an important genus for trout fishermen, but the larva, known as the green rock worm, is usually more important than the adult, especially to steelhead anglers. The larva is free-living in that it does not build a protective case, so it is unusually vulnerable to predation. In most areas of the West the emergence is not well organized. The worms live in fast pocket water, and the adults emerge and oviposit in the same areas. In situations in which trout are feeding on adults, those adults are usually egg-laying females. Some females ride the water quietly, some hop around, and some crawl underwater, so you will see both splashy and quiet riseforms. Fish will take wet and dry imitations. The adults seem to oviposit mainly on days with very little wind.

Little Brown Sedge
Family: Lepidostomatidae

Lepidostoma pluviale–Peak: Sporadic, mid-June–early September.

This caddisfly hatches from mid-June to early September, in the evening.

HOOK #18 (males one size smaller).

OVERALL LENGTH 10 millimeters.

BODY Bright olive.

Lepidostoma pluviale

WINGS Light brown. Males have a distinctive dark gray recurve on the leading edge of the wing, which can be used for identification.

LEGS Brown.

ANTENNAE Brown with lighter rings.

Lepidostoma case: This case is similar to the chimney cases of *Brachycentrus*, but its particles are wider.

Range: W, NW.

Habitat: Widespread.

Emergence: Evening, midstream.

Egg laying: On the surface, afternoon to evening.

Artificial flies: See page 101.

Lepidostoma case

This is an important species because it is widespread and has a long emergence period. It emerges from mid-June to early September in numbers only slightly smaller than those of the cinnamon sedge. Both the emergence and the egg-laying stages are important to the angler. After their evening emergence the adults ride the water for a relatively long time—10 to 20 seconds. Pupal, emerger, and adult patterns all take fish, but the pupal pattern seems to be most effective during the emergence. Both males and females ride the water in the resting position during egg laying, which occurs in the afternoon and evening.

Gray-Winged Long-Horn Sedge
Family: Leptoceridae

Oecetis disjuncta–Peak: June.

This caddisfly hatches from early June to late July, during warm summer afternoons and evenings, in all types of trout streams.

HOOK #16 (males one size smaller).

Oecetis disjuncta adult

OVERALL LENGTH 10–12 millimeters.

BODY Female–bright golden yellow; male–bright green.

WINGS Light gray. Long and slender.

LEGS Tan.

ANTENNAE Ginger with black rings; more than twice the body length.

Range: W, NW.

Habitat: Slow water.

Emergence: Late afternoon or evening in midstream.

Egg laying: On the surface.

Oecetis case

Artificial flies: See page 101.

This is an important species because its members hatch in the late spring and summer in the West and are large insects, which the trout seem to relish even when the peak emergence is over. They are on the wing when pale morning duns and green drakes are emerging and many anglers are at the river. These insects produce good rises, but anglers often overlook them to concentrate on the more popular mayflies. The fish often prefer the caddisflies.

Egg laying is the most important stage, but fish will feed on the emergers. Both emergence and ovipositing occur in late afternoon and evening. Both adults and spent imitations fished dead drift are effective. Medium to slow currents produce the larger hatches.

Note: The closely related tan-winged long-horn sedge (*Oecetis avara*) is less important, but can overlap the hatch of the gray-winged. Its behavior is similar; #16.

Black Dancer (Black Long-Horn Sedge)
Family: Leptoceridae

Mystacides alafimbriata–Peak: August.

This caddisfly hatches from late July to late August in slow water, morning and evening.

HOOK #18 (males one size smaller).

Mystacides alafimbriata

OVERALL LENGTH 9 millimeters.

BODY Black to dull amber.

WINGS Red-brown to black. Long and slender, abruptly bent together at tips.

LEGS Brown or dark gray.

ANTENNAE Black with light gray rings; more than twice the body length.

Range: W, NW.

Habitat: Slow water.

Emergence: Morning, mid-stream.

Mystacides case

Egg laying: Evening, midstream and near banks.

Artificial flies: See page 100.

This is an important species because its peak emergence in the West is in August, when insect activity is much lighter than in June and July. The caddisflies emerge in the morning from 7 to 10, when the temperature is cool and pleasant. Ovipositing is in the evening.

This fly rides the water serenely in a resting position for long distances. Trout take it quietly. Adult patterns are all you need, although trout will take the pupa at times.

Great Gray-Spotted Sedge
Family: Hydropsychidae

Arctopsyche grandis–Peak: Late June–July.

HOOK #8 (males one size smaller).

Arctopsyche grandis adult

OVERALL LENGTH 17–20 millimeters.

BODY Olive.

WINGS Grayish brown with light brown speckles.

LEGS Brown.

ANTENNAE Brown with darker rings.

Range: W.

Habitat: Trout rivers.

Emergence: Mainly at night.

Egg laying: Mainly at night.

Arctopsyche larva

The larval stage is by far the most important and can be used as a searching pattern during warm months. This caddisfly mainly emerges and lays eggs at night, which could be of interest to night fishermen.

Great Silver-Striped Sedge (Giant Golden Caddisfly)
Family: Limnephilidae

Hesperophylax designatus–Peak: Early July.

HOOK #8 (males one size smaller).

OVERALL LENGTH
17–20 millimeters.

BODY Bright olive.

WINGS Light ginger, with a silver stripe.

LEGS Ginger.

ANTENNAE Ginger.

Range: W.

Habitat: Trout rivers.

Emergence: Night.

Egg laying: Daytime.

The ovipositing stage of this species is significant to anglers. The females lay eggs close to banks, often skittering on the surface.

Hesperophylax designatus

Hesperophylax case

Giant Orange Sedge (October Caddisfly)
Family: Limnephilidae

Dicosmoecus atripes, D. gilvipes, D. juncundus–Peak: September–
October.

Dicosmoecus adult

Dicosmoecus case

HOOK #4–8.

OVERALL LENGTH
20–28 millimeters.

BODY Orange.

WINGS Gray with slight
mottling.

LEGS Tan.

ANTENNAE Tan.

Range: W, NW.

Habitat: Moderate to fast
water.

Emergence: In shallows,
evening.

Egg laying: At dusk, on the
surface.

Artificial flies: See page 102.

This is a most important genus for trout fishermen in the Pacific Northwest and Rocky Mountains. Every stage of this huge insect is taken by trout, and imitations of each stage are productive. The larvae exhibit behavioral drift in the summer, and unlike most aquatic insects this drift is in the daytime, so they are unusually vulnerable to predation.

The pupae migrate to the shallows in the fall before emerging in the late afternoon and evening. Ovipositing takes place at dusk and the females make quite a commotion, which attracts the attention of very large trout. Fishing a dry adult imitation with a pupa on a dropper in the shallows with a twitching retrieve can be very productive.

The Missouri River below Holter Dam has a good hatch of these caddisflies in September. Even during afternoons when only a few of these *Trichoptera* are flying, you can hear explosive rises. Trout in this river are on the lookout for these big flies, so the emergence does not need huge numbers of insects for you to enjoy very good angling.

Trout Lake Caddisflies

Lakes in which trout live must, obviously, provide food for those trout. Most of us think of damselflies, *Callibaetis* mayflies, midges, and scuds as primary sources of food. But caddisflies are also common in such lakes.

As it happens, the lakes that support trout are more common in the western United States and Canada than the East, probably because the high altitudes and latitudes here create the necessary low temperatures.

What we know about stillwater caddisflies has come primarily from entomologist Rick Hafele, who lives in Oregon and is also a serious angler. His observations are passed on here, partly from an article in *American Angler* magazine.

First, he tells us that caddisflies are better adapted to stillwater environments than are most mayflies or stoneflies. He points out that caddisflies living in lakes need the means to gather oxygen, since there is no current to bring it to them. Such caddisflies undulate their abdomens inside their cases to provide water flow over their gills, giving them a supply of oxygen.

There are three families of caddisflies that are best suited for living in lakes: the *Limnephilidae*, the *Leptoceridae*, and the *Phryganeidae*.

Trout Lake Caddisflies
Traveling Sedge

The hatch Rick finds most exciting is that of the *Banksiola crotchi*, of the family Phryganeidae. These are called traveling sedges, because they run across the surface to reach shore after emerging. The pupae swim up through open water to reach the lake's surface and shed their pupal shucks; then the adults run across the surface, leaving small wakes. Trout go crazy.

HOOK #8, 2XL.

BODY COLOR Dark olive.

WING COLOR Mottled gray.

PEAK Mid-June–mid-July.

Phryganeidae larva and case

Phryganeidae adult

Trout Lake Caddisflies
Tan Caddisfly

(To distinguish from the *Hydropsyche* cinnamon caddis.)

Regarding the Limnephilidae, Rick says that a few skitter across the surface at emergence, but most fly off the water. Both pupae and adults are taken readily by trout. The genus *Limnephilus*, which includes many species, is the most important of this family.

Limnephilidae larva

HOOK #12.

BODY COLOR Tan.

WING COLOR Mottled cinnamon.

Limnephilidae adult

Trout Lake Caddisflies
Black Dancer

Leptoceridae are interesting to Rick because the larvae of most species swim (and are eaten) in their cases, using their hind legs for propulsion. Evening is the normal time for species such as *Mystacides sepulchralis* to lay their eggs, by diving underwater. This is a close relative of the common black dancer known on western trout streams.

Rick says the black dancers are active in shallow water, in large numbers, both as emergers and egg layers. The Leptoceridae tend to be gray to shiny black, and are found in sizes 16 to 12. This entire family is noted by its designation as long-horn sedges.

HOOK #16–12.

Leptoceridae larva

BODY COLOR Dark gray.

WING COLOR Shiny black.

ANTENNAE Long ginger.

Leptoceridae adult

CHAPTER 5

Major Hatches East of the Mississippi

The hatch dates listed in this section are generally for New York through Michigan. In more southerly latitudes flies will hatch earlier; in more northerly latitudes, later.

As in the western chapter, the most important flies are color-coded—red, blue, and yellow—in order of importance. The hatches shown are roughly chronological, in the order of their peaks.

Black Caddisfly, Mother's Day Caddisfly
Family: Brachycentridae

*Brachycentrus americanus, B. lateralis, B. numerosus, B. appalachia,
B. solomoni, B. americanus*–Peak: Early April–mid-June.

This is the most important caddisfly in the spring.

These flies emerge in April and
May, at midday, from cold-
water trout streams and cold
tailwaters. Their characteristics
are:

Brachycentrus lateralis

HOOK #16 (males
one size smaller).

OVERALL LENGTH 9–13
millimeters.

BODY Dark gray with green or
tan lateral line.

WINGS Gray.

LEGS Gray.

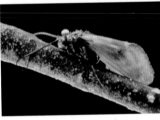

Brachycentrus americanus

ANTENNAE Dark gray with
lighter rings.

Note: *B. americanus* has a
brownish cast and is larger
than *B. lateralis*.

B. lateralis case

B. numerosus case

B. americanus case

Brachycentrus case: The case of the little black caddisfly is known as a chimney case. It has a square cross section and is tapered. The cases can be found clinging to stones and wood, and they are numerous before the hatch. (The *B. numerosus* case is tubular at the bottom, and only square at the top.) When checking cases, be sure to note whether they contain larvae or not, because empty cases last quite a while and their presence can be misleading.

Range: NE, SE, M.

Habitat: Coid trout streams.

Emergence: Midday, midstream.

The pupae often drift many feet attached to the surface film before emerging.

Egg laying: Midday and afternoon, midstream.

Artificial flies: See page 100.

Black Caddisfly, Mother's Day Caddisfly

This is the year's first heavy emergence of caddisflies in the East, and trout feed heavily on it. The hatch usually occurs on un-dammed trout streams and bottom-release tailwaters. The flies begin emerging around midday, just as the hendrickson hatch is waning. Egg laying is in the afternoon and can coincide with the emergence. Peak emergence occurs from the last half of April to mid-June, on balmy days. The adults drift up to 30 feet struggling from their pupal shucks. Once out, they may drift on the surface or fly away quickly. They oviposit much like mayflies, dipping their bodies onto the surface, although some individuals may crawl or dive underwater.

Brachycentrus pupa

Cinnamon Caddisfly, Tan Caddisfly
Family: Hydropsychidae

Hydropsyche morosa, H. sparna, H. slossonae, et al.–Peak: All season.

This family is the most important in the summer months.

*Hydropsyche
(Ceratopsyche) adult*

These flies emerge from May to September, mainly in the evening in summer, but some earlier in the day. They are most important in tailwaters, but some are found in trout streams. Their characteristics are:

HOOK #16 (males one size smaller).

**OVERALL
LENGTH**
9–15 millimeters.

BODY Cinnamon brown.

WINGS Brownish gray with a speckling of small tan spots.

LEGS Brown.

ANTENNAE Tan with dark wings.

*Hydropsyche larva
(note three plates behind head)*

Hydropsyche larva: This larva is characterized by three hard, dark plates on the body segments behind its head, as are its relatives in the family Hydropsychidae. Bodies are tan or gray.

It builds a net like a spiderweb among the gravel to trap food. It does not build a case until it is ready to pupate, about two weeks before emergence.

Range: NE, SE, M.

Habitat: Mainly tailwaters, but also widespread.

Emergence: Morning, afternoon, and evening, midstream.

The pupa often drifts many feet attached to the surface film before emerging.

Egg laying: Morning and evening: swimming or crawling underwater.

Artificial flies: See pages 101 and 103–106.

This is by far the most important family for trout fishermen. Only in the early spring when little black caddisflies and tiny black caddisflies are on the water do any other caddisflies even come close in importance to this fly and its cousin, the little olive caddisfly.

They hatch in large numbers, usually in the evening but also in the morning, seemingly when the nights are very warm. Egg laying is done in the morning and evening, with some during the day.

These caddisflies drift as pupae for a long time before their emergence. They also take a long time to struggle from their pupal shucks. These two factors allow you to hook a lot of fish long before the hatch begins on a pupal imitation fished dead drift on the bottom, as a floating pupa just under the surface film, or as an emerger. The pupae emerge in midstream.

The females crawl or dive underwater or sprawl on the surface to lay eggs. A surface-fished dry fly is often effective during egg laying, or it can be pulled under the surface to imitate the returning egg-laying female.

Many spent caddisflies collect on the water after dark, and the fish will feed selectively on quad-wing patterns at that time.

To find out which stage of the insect the fish are taking, tie on a floating fly, tie a dropper from it, and attach a pupal imitation, which will float just under the surface. Fish these dead drift. If the fish take one consistently you know which fly to use.

If the fish rise all around your flies but do not take, pull the dry fly underwater. It may then be taken for an egg-laying female returning to the surface.

At the end of egg laying, fish will often take a spent imitation. A quad-wing fly or delta-wing fly will then work.

Note: Those caddisflies that do not live in cases as larvae—such as this one—build cases briefly for a couple of weeks to change into pupae. You can easily tell one of these pupal cases from the normal larval case because it is open on one side. When you take a knife and remove it from a rock, the entire pupa, enclosed in a silk sac, is exposed as if in a window (see illustration).

Temporary case (open on the bottom, attached to rock)

Little Olive Caddisfly (Little Sister Sedge)
Family: Hydropsychidae

Cheumatopsyche speciosa, C. analis, C. lasia, C. campyla, C. harwoodi—Peak: All season.

Cheumatopsyche adult

These flies emerge from May to September, mainly during the evening in summer, but some earlier in the day (in September, they emerge in the morning). They are most important in tailwaters, but some are found in trout streams. Their characteristics are:

HOOK #18
(males one size
smaller).

OVERALL LENGTH
7.5 millimeters.

BODY Olive.

WINGS Brownish gray with a speckling of small tan markings.

LEGS Brown.

ANTENNAE Tan with dark rings.

Cheumatopsyche larva: This larva is characterized by three dark plates on the body segments behind the head, as are its relatives in the family Hydropsychidae. Bodies are green to olive.

Cheumatopsyche larva

It builds a net like a spiderweb among the gravel to trap food. it does not build a case until it is ready to pupate, about two weeks before emergence.

Range: NE, SE, M.

Habitat: Riffles in warm tailwaters.

Emergence: Afternoon and evening in midstream.

Temporary case (open on the bottom, attached to rock)

The pupa often drifts many feet just under the surface film before emerging.

Egg laying: Swims or crawls underwater.

Artificial flies: See page 101.

This is the second most important genus for trout fishermen, a close second to *Hydropsyche*, to which it is clearly related. Since these genera belong to the same family their habits, style of emergence, and egg laying are very similar, if not identical. They hatch and lay eggs at the same time of day, interspersed with the cinnamon caddis hatch.

These insects are similar in shape to cinnamon caddis and have the same unique wing shape. They are a little smaller than *Hydropsyche* and can easily be distinguished from them by their smaller size and olive body color. The few *Hydropsyche* that have olive bodies at emergence (which quickly turn cinnamon or brown) are larger. These caddisflies become much lighter as the season progresses—as do many other species, but the little olive seems to exhibit this trait in the extreme. The wings, which are dark in the early season, become much lighter in fall and appear white in flight. They are usually evening emergers in the summer, but some switch to morning emergence in the fall.

The females dive underwater or sprawl on the surface to lay eggs. A surface-fished dry fly is often effective during egg laying, or it can be pulled under the surface to imitate the returning egg-laying female.

Many spent caddisflies collect on the water after dark, and the fish will feed selectively on quad-wing patterns at that time.

Dark Blue Sedge
(East and Appalachia only)
Family: Odontoceridae

Psilotreta labida, P. frontalis—Peak: Late April-mid-June.

These flies emerge from late April to mid-June, in the evening, on all types of trout streams. Their characteristics are:

HOOK #14
(males one size
smaller).

OVERALL LENGTH
12–15 millimeters.

BODY Green to almost black.

WINGS Dark grayish brown
with small light spots.

Psilotreta frontalis

LEGS Very dark gray.

ANTENNAE Black.

Psilotreta case

Range: NE, SE.

Habitat: On rocks in moderate riffles.

Emergence: Evening.

Egg laying: On the surface, in the evening.

Artificial flies: See page 102.

These are important species in the East and mid-South from late April to June. They emerge in the evening. The pupae swim to the surface to emerge, and females flop on the surface to oviposit, both in the evening. Trout are attracted to this commotion, and dry imitations work best.

Green Sedge (Green Rock Worm)
Family: Rhyacophilidae

Rhyacophila fuscula (East); *R. melita, R. manistee* (Midwest); *R. fuscula, R. vuphipes* (South)—Peak: Sporadic; spring to fall.

These caddisflies hatch spring to fall in the evening from fast, cold trout streams.

HOOK #14
(males one size
smaller).

Rhyacophila melita

OVERALL LENGTH 12–15 millimeters, a few species to 18 millimeters.

BODY Green.

WINGS Grayish brown, mottled.

LEGS Tan.

ANTENNAE Tan with darker bands.

Range: NE, SE, M.

Habitat: Cold-water riffles.

Green Sedge
(Green Rock Worm)

Emergence: Afternoon, from riffles.

Egg laying: Crawls or swims to the bottom in riffles.

Artificial flies: See page 101.

The green rock worm. Note the one hard plate behind the head—a characteristic of the *Rhyacophila*.

This is an important genus for trout fishermen, but the larva, known as the green rock worm, is usually more important than the adult. The larva is free-living in that it does not build a protective case, so it is unusually vulnerable to predation. In most areas emergence is not heavily concentrated. The worms live in fast pocket water, and the adults emerge and oviposit in the same areas. In situations in which trout are feeding on adults, those adults are usually egg-laying females. Some females ride the water quietly, some hop around, and some crawl underwater, so you will see both splashy and quiet riseforms. Fish will take wet and dry imitations. The adults seem to oviposit mainly on days with very little wind.

Tiny Black Caddisfly (Short-Horn Sedge)
Family: Glossosomatidae

Glossosoma nigrior–Peak: Spring mornings.

These flies emerge sporadically from spring to fall in trout streams, occasionally in large numbers, usually in the morning.

HOOK #20 (males one size smaller).

OVERALL LENGTH 6–7.5 millimeters.

BODY Black.

WINGS Black with a few light tan spots midwing, and a few at the wing tips.

Glossosoma nigrior

LEGS Dark gray.

ANTENNAE Black.

Glossosoma case: This case is known as a domed saddle case. The larva takes the case with it as it moves along the surface of rocks.

Glossosoma case

Range: NE, M.

Habitat: Cold streams.

Emergence: Riffles in midstream, crawling to the banks.

Egg laying: Submerges in riffles.

Artificial flies: See page 100.

This is an important species because its members emerge all season long, usually a few at a time but occasionally in good numbers. They can cause heavy feeding when the emergence is large, and some rises when the hatch is light. Since these are small, dark forms, they are hard to see, but fish will feed on them. (You may notice that the trout are rising, but see nothing on the water.) The most important time for this hatch is during spring mornings, because not much else is emerging at this time.

The pupae emerge in midstream, and pupal and emerger imitations are effective. In the spring some pupae emerge in midstream and crawl on the surface of the water to shore. A hackled pupal imitation skittered on the surface is very effective at these times. Females submerge to oviposit.

Tiny Black Caddisfly
Family: Brachycentridae

Micrasema scotti (E & S); *M. rusticam* (M)—Peak: April–mid-May;
September–October.

HOOK #20 (males
one size smaller).

OVERALL LENGTH
7–9 millimeters.

BODY Dark gray with green or
tan lateral line.

WINGS Black.

Micrasema rusticum

LEGS Dark gray.

ANTENNAE Dark gray with
lighter rings.

Range: NE, SE, M.

Habitat: Cold streams.

Emergence: Morning and
evening.

Egg laying: Morning and evening.

Micrasema case

Artificial flies: See page 100.

These are important species because the peak emergence in the East and Midwest is concentrated. Although hard to see, the insects hatch in large numbers to emerge and oviposit during mornings and evenings. These insects ride the water for only a very short time, so pupal patterns are much more effective than emergers or adults.

Females lay their eggs on the river bottom. They then swim back to the surface, floating awash in the film, where spentwing imitations are the most effective, fished dry. Adult imitations are effective fished wet. Some individuals may dip their eggs on the surface.

On some very cold tailwaters, such as the South Holston of Tennessee, there are spring and fall emergences of *M. scotti*.

Zebra Caddisfly
Family: Hydropsychidae

Macrostemum zebratum–Peak: Mid-summer evenings.

HOOK #12
(males one size
larger).

OVERALL LENGTH
15–18 millimeters.

BODY Freshly emerged–green,
black ribbing; later–black body,
yellow ribbing.

Macrostemum zebratum

WINGS Ginger, black markings
as shown.

LEGS Yellow.

ANTENNAE Very long, black.

Range: NE, SE, M.

Habitat: Warm trout rivers.

Emergence: Warm summer
evenings.

Egg laying: Dives or sprawls in
the evening and after dark.

Macrostemum larva

This is an important caddisfly in the East, Midwest, and Southeast because it is a large insect, its emergence and egg-laying flights are often huge, and it appears during warm summer evenings when many anglers are fishing. These insects are not found on very cold trout streams, but most of our warmer rivers, like the Housatonic in Connecticut and the Muskegon in Michigan, have large hatches. When these insects are on the water trout will not refuse a well-tied imitation. Some females crawl underwater to oviposit; others dive from high in the air, hit the water, and either sprawl on the surface or actually dive underwater to oviposit. It has been written that many species of caddisflies dive underwater for egg laying, but this is one of the few species we have actually observed doing so.

The larvae are fat and meaty and are available for predation when drifting. An imitation of this stage, fished on the bottom, is a good searching pattern in the spring and summer.

Tan-Winged Long-Horn Sedge
Family: Leptoceridae

Oecetis avara–Peak: Warm summer evenings.

This insect hatches from late May to September during warm summer evenings, in all types of trout streams.

HOOK #16 (males one size larger).

OVERALL LENGTH 10–12 millimeters.

BODY Female–dull yellow; male–olive.

WINGS Tan. Long and slender.

LEGS Ginger.

ANTENNAE Ginger, with dark bands; more than twice the body length.

Range: NE, SE, M.

Habitat: Slow water.

Emergence: Warm summer afternoons and evenings, edges and slow water.

Oecetis avara

Oecetis case

Egg laying: On the surface and edges, in slow water.

Artificial flies: See page 101.

This is an important species because its members fly almost all summer on warm evenings, are fairly large, and can emerge in huge numbers. Like all the species in this family, they have antennae 2.5 times the length of their bodies. The pupae swim to the surface to emerge, and the adults sprawl on the surface or dive underwater to oviposit. Emergence is during warm afternoons and evenings. When trout feed on this species they generally take adults on the surface, although they do take pupae as well.

Note: The closely related brown long-horn sedge (*Oecetis inconspicua*) is less important, but can overlap the hatch of the tan-winged. Its behavior is similar; #16.

Dark Long-Horn Sedge
Family: Leptoceridae

Ceraclea transversa–Peak: Midsummer evenings, after dark.

HOOK #16 (males one size larger).

OVERALL LENGTH 11–16 millimeters.

BODY Dark red-brown to black.

WINGS Red-brown to brownish gray, often with pale markings.

Ceraclea adult

LEGS Brown or dark gray.

ANTENNAE Brown to black; more than twice the body length.

Range: NE, SE, M.

Habitat: Widespread.

Ceraclea case

Emergence: Warm summer evenings, midstream.

Egg laying: On the surface.

Artificial flies: See page 100.

This is an important species because its members fly almost all summer on warm evenings, are fairly large, and can emerge in huge numbers. They have antennae 2.5 times the length of their bodies. The pupae swim to the surface to emerge, and the adults sprawl on the surface or dive underwater to oviposit. Emergence is during warm evenings and after dark. When trout feed on this species they generally take adults on the surface, although they do take the pupae as well.

White Miller (White Long-Horn Sedge)
Family: Leptoceridae

Nectopsyche albida, N. exquisita–Peak: Evening; August–September.

HOOK #16 (males one size larger).

Nectopsyche albida

OVERALL LENGTH 10--11 millimeters.

BODY Light olive.

WINGS Cream. Long and slender.

LEGS Ginger.

ANTENNAE White with tan rings; more than twice the body length.

Range: NE, SE, M.

Habitat: Riffles, slow water.

Emergence: Midstream, at and after dark.

Nectopsyche case

Egg laying: Riffles, in the evening.

Artificial flies: See page 102.

These are important species because they fly midsummer to fall on warm evenings, are fairly large, and can emerge in huge numbers. Due to its color, the white miller is a conspicuous insect. It emerges in the evening and after dusk in large numbers. Both the emergence and the egg-laying stages are important to the angler. The pupae swim to the surface to emerge. Females submerge or sprawl on the surface to oviposit in late evening and after dark.

Dot-Winged Sedge
Large Dot-Winged Sedge
Family: Limnephilidae

Frenesia missa, F. difficilis—Peak: October, in the East.

HOOK #16 (males one size smaller).

OVERALL LENGTH *F. missa*— 12 millimeters; *F. difficilis*— 15 millimeters.

BODY Dark gray with light tan lateral line.

WINGS Dark brown with many small, light tan dots.

LEGS Brownish yellow.

ANTENNAE Brownish yellow and white with tan rings.

Frenesia adult

Frenesia case

Small Dot-Winged Sedge
Family: Uenoidae

Neophylax fuscus–Peak: September–October, in the Midwest.

HOOK #18
(males one
size smaller).

OVERALL LENGTH
11 millimeters.

Neophylax case

Dot-Winged Sedges

Range: NE, M.

Emergence: In the shallows, daytime.

Egg laying: Near shore.

Artificial flies: See page 100.

These are important species for fall trout fishermen. The pupae emerge in the daytime by crawling to the shallows to hatch. Pupal imitations fished slow and deep are effective, as are adults fished dry. Adults oviposit near shore. Because adult imitations are so effective, it is possible that some females submerge to oviposit.

These insects can come in large numbers, especially on warm, sunny fall days, and since not much else is emerging at this time, fish feed voraciously on them.

N. fuscus is a common and important fall caddisfly in the Midwest. It looks very much like a Brachycentridae in the hand, but the only genus of Brachycentridae that emerges in the fall is *Microsema*, which does not have the small light dots on the wings.

Great Brown Autumn Sedge
Family: Limnephilidae

Pycnopsyche guttifer, P. lepida–Peak: Late August–September.

Pycnopsyche lepida

HOOK #8 (males one size smaller).

OVERALL LENGTH 19–21 millimeters.

BODY Ginger.

WINGS Yellowish brown with two conspicuous black marks.

LEGS Ginger.

ANTENNAE Black.

Range: NE, M.

Habitat: Logs along edges.

Emergence: Mainly at night.

Egg laying: Mainly at night, occasionally afternoon.

The cases of these caddisflies can be easily spotted by looking on logs around the edge of the stream. The insects are nighttime emergers, with occasional activity at first light or in the afternoon.

Pycnopsyche case

You can often see large numbers flying around grassy areas nears trout streams on sunny afternoons in the fall. They are so large that when we first noticed them, we thought they were butterflies.

CHAPTER 6

Tying Caddisfly Imitations

Because the behavior of the caddisflies is complex, tying effective imitations of them requires using some different forms.

Any fly pattern is subject to infinite variation and creativity of course, so go to it at your tying bench and experiment on the river. Our objective is to provide one basic, simple pattern for each of the major stages of the caddisfly.

The hook sizes we refer to are based on the following brands and styles:

Orvis	1523 (Big Eye 1639)
Tiemco	5210
Daiichi	1180
Mustad	94840

Different tyers might use different sizes of hooks, because of different perceptions of sizes, or different ratios of body length to wing length. The overall length of most caddisfly adults is 1.4 times the body length (inversely, the body is 0.7 times the overall length). A few variations are mentioned in the text. We have also noted that males are normally one size smaller than females. Since females are on the water more, we usually start our fishing with that size of artificial, but males can be important at hatch time and as spent flies after mating.

The patterns here are based on the cinnamon caddisfly, the olive caddisfly, and the black caddisfly. Most caddisflies can be imitated with a variation of these three. The individual descriptions of each hatch include depictions of the varying colors you can use for imitation. For color, then, use the pictures and descriptions in the text.

The patterns are listed in order of the life cycle of the caddisfly. First is the free larva.

Since the larva drifts with its head down, it should be imitated with the pattern we call the Beadhead-Down. The fly is tied backward, on a curved caddis hook. The bead is dark, and tied to form the head.

Beadhead Down Larva

Hook Heavy-wire shrimp/caddis hook, #16.
Body Olive Body Stretch over hare's ear dubbing.
Ribbing Fine copper wire.
Antenna None.
Legs Partridge.
Head Black bead.

This fly should be fished near the bottom with a strike indicator, lifting slightly to give the fly up-and-down motion, but otherwise dead-drifted.

Deep-Drifting Pupa

Hook Heavy-wire shrimp/caddis hook, #16.
Body Ginger Antron dubbing.
Dorsal Ribbing Dark brown marking pen.
Legs Mallard duck flank, dyed brown.
Antennae None.
Wings Dark brown quill.
Head Dark brown Antron dubbing.

This fly should be fished dead drift along the bottom, then tugged gradually toward the surface with a twitching motion, to give motion to its swimming legs. It should not be tied with a beadhead, which would keep the body from drifting horizontally.

Emerging Pupa

Hook Light-wire Orvis Big Eye, 1639, #16.
Body Ginger Antron dubbing.
Legs Mallard flank feathers, dyed brown.
Hackle Light dun.
Wings (flotation) Snowshoe rabbit foot.
Rib Krystal Flash.

We have found that using a sparse parachute hackle with snowshoe rabbit foot in place of a wing floats this fly best. This is for flotation only, and to keep the body just under the surface.

This fly should float right under the surface film dead drift, or it may be fished as a dropper behind an emerger or adult pattern. Some people find that this is often as effective as an emerger pattern.

Teardrop Emerger

Hook Light-wire Orvis Big Eye, #16.
Shuck Ginger Z-Lon.
Body Ginger Antron.
Wing Snowshoe rabbit.
Hackle None.

This is a simplified teardrop emerger pattern. It is usually fished dead drift on the surface, with occasional tiny twitches.

Adult Caddis

Hook Light-wire Orvis Big Eye, #16.
Body Ginger cream Fly Rite.
Wings Mottled tan Fly Film.
Hackle Ginger.
Antennae Tan.

This pattern may be tied in many ways. We have found Fly Film or Aire-Flow to be the simplest. The choice depends on the color and pattern. Fly Film is good when a clear or marked wing is called for; Aire-Flow has some good mottled colors. A light dressing of elk hair or coastal deer hair can be tied as an overwing to add flotation. Taped or coated wings can also be used.

This fly can be fished as a dead-drifting adult, as a returning egg layer—under the surface—or as a skittered fly. Skittering is accomplished by wiggling the rod tip horizontally.

Spentwing Caddis

Hook Light-wire Orvis Big Eye, #16.
Body Ginger cream Fly Rite.
Wings Tan poly yarn.
Legs None.
Antennae Tan.

This fly is usually fished after dark, dead drift, on calm, flat water. The spent caddisflies fall to the water after their final egg laying and are easy prey for fish, which feed with extreme selectivity after dark. We have mentioned that at such times it may be necessary to pick the site of the last rise, drift your fly to that spot, then set the hook before seeing a rise.

CHAPTER 7

Master List of Major Caddis Patterns

This list will cover most of the natural caddisflies you're likely to see on trout streams in numbers that would cause selective feeding by trout. The most important hatches are marked with an asterisk.

Each pattern and size can be tied in an adult, pupa, larva, or spentwing version, as needed.

1. **Black Caddis**	Common hook size
*Brachycentrus**	#16
Micrasema	#20
Amiocentrus	#20
Glossosoma	#20
Mystacides	#16 (Long-horn, long wing)
Ceraclea	#14 (Long-horn, long wing)
Neophylax	#18

Materials:

Body Dark gray dubbing.

Wings Black or gray hen hackle on Scotch tape, cemented, folded, and clipped to shape.

2. **Green Sedge**   Common hook size

    Rhyacophila   #14

    *Cheumatopsyche**   #18

    Lepidostoma   #16

Materials:

Body Olive green dubbing.

Wings Brown speckled partridge back feathers on
Scotch tape, cemented, folded, and clipped to shape.

Hackle Brown.

---

3. **Cinnamon Caddis**   Common hook size

    *Hydropsyche**   #16

    Helicopsyche   #20

Materials:

Body Cinnamon dubbing.

Wings Brown speckled partridge back feathers
on Scotch tape, cemented, folded, and clipped to shape.

Hackle Light brown.

---

4. **Tan- or Gray-winged
Long-Horn Sedge**   Common hook size

    Oecetis   #16 (Long-horn, long wing)

Materials:

Body Tan and olive; ginger thorax.

Wings Tan hen body feather on Scotch tape, cemented,
folded, and clipped to shape (slim).

Hackle Tan.

5. **White Miller**   Common hook size
    Nectopsyche   #16 (Long-horn)
Materials:
Body Olive with tan thorax.
Wings Cream hen body feather on Scotch tape,
cemented, folded, and clipped to shape (slim).
Hackle Ginger.

---

6. **Dark Blue Sedge**   Common hook size
    Psilotreta*   #14
Materials:
Body Dark gray to dark green.
Wings Dark gray hen body feather on Scotch tape,
cemented, folded, and clipped to shape.
Hackle Dark gray.

---

7. **Giant Orange Sedge**   Common hook size
    Dicosmoecus   #4–8
Materials:
Body Orange dubbing.
Wings Gray hen body feather on Scotch tape, cemented,
folded, and clipped to shape.
Hackle Rusty brown.

You can see that you need only seven patterns in a
few sizes to match all the important flies.

Tying the Tape-and-Feather-Winged Cinnamon Caddis

(A more exact imitation of the natural.)

This pattern is effective fished either wet or dry during egg laying. Skittering it on the surface is sometimes deadly—especially if females are swimming back to the surface, bouncing on the surface before flying off to mate again, and returning to the river to lay more eggs. It will catch fish during an emergence, but usually the emerger or pupa is better at that time.

Hook #16–18, 3X fine wire. Males are usually one size smaller than females. (This is true except for long-horn and zebra caddis, which are one size larger.) The bodies of caddisflies are shorter than the wings, so an imitation tied on a #16 hook will look like a #14 insect. It is important not to tie these patterns too large.

Body Fine-textured cinnamon dubbing. You'll also want to carry a few in yellow and olive.

Antennae Two stripped hackle quills, deer or moose hair, flank feathers from mallard or wood ducks (optional—they make the fly look a lot better but are fragile). Guard hairs from mink tails and various other animals are the most durable, as well as synthetic fibers.

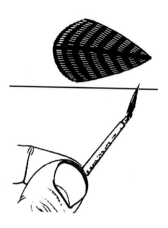

Paint the taped feather with flexible cement.

Wings Black and flank feathers from various birds.
Quail, grouse, and plain and variegated hen hack-
les are ideal for this fly. Press the feathers onto
Scotch tape, then coat the feather side with Seal-
All, a flexible cement, and let dry. Fold the coated
feathers in the middle at the stem to form the
wings. Next, clip them to the selected wing shape
and tie in.

Thin, clear packaging tape can also be used.
This is more flexible than Scotch Tape, so it makes
for a softer wing. Alternate wing materials are:
coastal deer hair, hackle tips, and poly yarn.

The wings of caddisflies have a sheen that hair
and feathers do not. This sheen can be added to
hair wings by tying a few fibers of Z-Lon or poly
yarn under the wing. The cement-coated gamebird

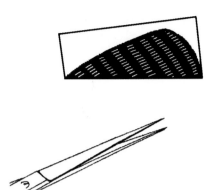

Fold the taped feather in the middle and trim to shape.

feathers get their sheen from the cement and/or the tape. The wings of these insects are lighter than they look when you study them in the hand. If you hold a natural up to the sky and observe it from underneath, you will notice the wings are translucent and appear lighter than when you look at them from the top. This is how the trout see them—from underneath. It is important to use a material that is not too dark.

Hackle Reddish brown hackle tied in before or after the wing, and clipped on top and bottom. Hackle is optional, as the pattern works quite well without it, but it does ensure that the fly lands upright. Hackle can also be tied in parachute-style; such flies are great for skittering. The post for the parachute is

This is the correct wing shape for all the
Cinnamon Caddis and Little Olive Caddis imitations

round rubber, sold in fly shops. It is tied in on the
top of the head and stretched. We use a gallows
tool and hackle pliers to hold the stretched rubber.
After the hackle is wound around the stretched
rubber and tied down, the rubber post is clipped
while still stretched close to the top of the hackle
bunch. The rubber post will pull down and lock the
hackle firmly into place. Doug Swisher invented
this method of tying parachute hackle.

CHAPTER 8

Occasionally Important Caddisflies

Name		Hook Size
Tiny Black Caddisfly *Chimarra aterrima* Philopotamidae		#20
Black Gold-Spotted Caddisfly *Dolophilodes distinctus* Philopotamidae		#20
Tiny Dark Eastern Woodland Sedge *Lype diversa* Psychomyiidae		#22
Brown-Checkered Summer Sedge *Polycentropus cinereus* Polycentropodidae		#18
Dinky Purple-Breasted Sedge *Psychomyia flavida* Psychomyiidae		#22
Giant Cream Pattern-Winged Sedge *Hydatophylax argus* Limnephilidae		#8

Name		Hook Size
Chocolate & Cream Sedge *Platycentropus radiatus* Limnephilidae		#8
Little Gray Sedge *Goera calcarata* Limnephilidae		#18
Summer Flyer, Tan Caddisfly *Limnephilus sericus,* *L. submonilifer* Limnephilidae		#14
Early Smoky-Winged Sedge *Apatania incerta* Limnephilidae		#20
Dinky Light Summer Sedge *Nyctiophylax moestus* Limnephilidae		#20
Gray-Checkered Sedge *Molanna cinera,* *M. uniophila* Molannidae		#14

Bibliography

Flint, O. S. Jr. 1984. The Genus *Brachycentrus* in North America, with a Proposed Phylogeny of the Genera of Brachycentridae (Trichoptera). Smithsonian Institution Press, *Smithsonian Contributions to Zoology* Number 398.

Hafele, Rick, and Dave Hughes. *The Complete Book of Western Hatches*. Portland, OR: Frank Amato Publications, 1987.

Hughes, David, *Western Streamside Guide*. Portland, OR: Frank Amato Publications, 1987.

Juracek, John, and Craig Mathews. *Fishing the Yellowstone Hatches*. West Yellowstone, MT: Blue Ribbon Flies, 1992.

LaFontaine, Gary. *Caddisflies*. New York, NY: Lyons & Burford, 1981.

Leonard, J. W., and F. A. Leonard. 1949. An Annotated List of Michigan Trichoptera. *Occasional Papers of the Museum of Zoology, University of Michigan*, 522.

_____ 1949. Noteworthy Records of Caddis Flies from Michigan with Descriptions of New Species. *Papers of the Museum of Zoology, University of Michigan*.

McCafferty, W. Patrick. *Aquatic Entomology.* Boston, MA: Jones and Bartlett, 1981.

Merritt, R. W., K. W. Cummins, and M. B. Berq, editors. *An Introduction to the Aquatic Insects of North America*, 4th edition. Dubuque, IA: Kendall/Hunt Publishing Col., 1978.

Richards, Carl, and Braendle, Robert. *Caddis Super Hatches.* Portland, OR: Frank Amato Publications, 1997.

Ross, H. H. 1944. The Caddisflies, or Trichoptera, of Illinois. *State of Ill. Natural History Survey Division*, Volume 23.

Ross, H. H., and J. D. Unzicker, 1965. The *Micrasema rusticum* Group of Caddisflies (Brachycentridae, Trichoptera). *Proceedings of the Biological Society of Washington* 78:251-258.

Shewey, John. *Mastering the Spring Creeks.* Portland, OR: Frank Amato Publications, 1994.

Solomon, Larry, and Eric Leiser. *The Caddis and the Angler.* Harrisburg, PA: Stackpole Books, 1977.

Wiggins, G. B. *Larvae of the North American Caddisfly Genera (Trichoptera)*, 2nd edition. Toronto, Canada and Buffalo, NY: University of Toronto Press, 1996.

Photographic Credits

A book like this would have been impossible without the wonderful illustrations and photographs from all the contributors listed below.

Alecia Richards: v (In Memoriam)

Carl Richards: 7, 23, 25b, 27, 38t, 41
61t, 61b, 63, 64, 68, 73, 79, 81, 83,
85, 87, 90, 94, 95, 96, 97.

Dave Hughes: 28b, 44, 54, 74.

Jim Schollmeyer: 6, 10, 29, 38b, 43b,
57t, 57b, 58t, 58b, 59t, 59b.

John Juracek: 25t, 28t, 33, 36, 43t, 45,
47, 49, 51, 53, 77.

Hank Leonard: 13, 99.

Thomas Ames Jr.: 12, 71, 75.

Robert McKeon created the line drawings and silhouettes in this book.

Personal Hatch Record

Caddisfly Hatches of _____

Importance	Latin Name	Common Name	Hook #	Mar	Apr	May	

June	July	Aug	Sep	Oct	Nov	Emergence	Ovipositing

Personal Hatch Record

Caddisfly Hatches of _____

Importance	Latin Name	Common Name	Hook #	Mar	Apr	May	

	June	July	Aug	Sep	Oct	Nov	Emergence	Ovipositing

Personal Hatch Record

Caddisfly Hatches of _____

Importance	Latin Name	Common Name	Hook #	Mar	Apr	May	

	June	July	Aug	Sep	Oct	Nov	Emergence	Ovipositing

Personal Hatch Record

Caddisfly Hatches of _____

Importance	Latin Name	Common Name	Hook #	Mar	Apr	May	

June	July	Aug	Sep	Oct	Nov	Emergence	Ovipositing

Personal Hatch Record

Caddisfly Hatches of _____

Importance	Latin Name	Common Name	Hook #	Mar	Apr	May	

June	July	Aug	Sep	Oct	Nov	Emergence	Ovipositing

Personal Hatch Record

Caddisfly Hatches of _____

Importance	Latin Name	Common Name	Hook #	Mar	Apr	May	

June	July	Aug	Sep	Oct	Nov	Emergence	Ovipositing

Index